David Maclagan

creation myths

Man's introduction to the world

With 149 illustrations, 19 in color

Thames and Hudson

Art and Imagination
General Editor: Jill Purce

Reprinted 1979

Library of Congress Catalog card number 78–63581

Printed in Singapore

Contents

In memory of my mothers

Man's introduction to the world

'In the beginning' is a forefather of 'once upon a time': it is the passport to a realm which is shadowy and speculative, more or less fabulous, in character. It implies a fantastic ambition: to account for the origin of the world and the nature of everything that follows from it; to make visible (for that is the root meaning of 'fantasy') what must, by definition, be invisible to men: the moment or process of their own creation. What is this 'creation'? how do we arrive at the notion 'in the first place'? It is the vanishing-point with which we are faced when we trace *everything-that-is* back to *something-that-was*, and, reaching beyond that, to *nothing-that-was-not*. Such is the usual order of our thinking: in most accounts of creation, however, this perspective is apparently reversed.

The sheer scale of this riddle might seem to make it a matter for special, exceptional attention; but creation is not only cosmogonic, but onto-genetic: in other words, it is invoked whenever any new thing – from the quickening of an embryo to the dawning of an image – is brought to life. The great creation accounts, such as the Hebrew *Genesis*, the Babylonian *Enuma Elish* or the Mayan *Popul Vuh*, deal with the cosmogonic scenario directly and explicitly; but the origin of any thing (and hence, of things in general) is implicit in almost all explanation or definition: every 'how' entails a 'why'.

The origin of things is their *foundation*; it is what their existence has been built upon. Therefore we can never encounter their original nature directly; there is a fundamental discrepancy, a postponement, between us and the 'beginning'. Hence, for example, the distinction made in Pytha-gorean/Orphic thought between the principle *behind* the cosmos and the causes obtaining *within* it: number, the cosmic 'law', is seen as the interface between these, between infinite and finite. The only basis we have for describing what was, or is, behind existence is in terms of what has already been derived from that primal creative process: terms which are thus 'second-hand' or symbolic. The eighteenth-century philosopher Lichtenberg once suggested:

> If a higher being were ever to tell us about the origin of the world, I wonder whether we should be capable of understanding him. . . . It may well be that outside our minds there is nothing whatever corresponding to our conception of origin, the moment it is applied, not to the relation of things with other things, but to the things themselves.

The paradox appears as a 'No Entry' sign, which we can evade only by breaking the normal rules of explanation: as when we resort to myth.

The problem is compounded by the existence of myth itself as a creation – and by the widespread suspicion that it is a fictitious and misleading one, which men have fabricated in order to hoist themselves up by their own bootstraps and explain the inexplicable. The very phrase 'creation myth' conjures up the possibility that the two senses of 'creation' – the cosmogonic and the imaginative – may somehow have got confused, so that what we, like Narcissus, take to be something quite other turns out to be our own image in reflection. And it is true that the realms of 'nature' and 'culture', which we tend for the sake of convenience to see as mutually exclusive (the unalterable 'laws of nature' versus the arbitrary rules of society, for example) do interpenetrate; and myth is one of the forms in which the mapping of each on the other can be seen at its highest density. This interweaving – which is not only of nature and culture but also of subject and object – is something we find hard to tolerate, because the framework of our most authoritative forms of knowledge (the strictest types of physics, philosophy and psychology, for example) is founded upon scrupulous discrimination between these very categories. The fine, close-up focus that this calls for requires a strict adherence to what Wittgenstein called 'the logic of representation'; a logic which seeks to purge language-use of all ambiguity or multivalence, to disinfect meaning of metaphoric contamination. But (as Wittgenstein himself showed) these strictures also result in a loss of depth and in the virtual evaporation of most of the questions that really concern us in life.

We cannot get rid of the harmonic undertones and overtones of language, the rich resonance of human discourse: it is significant that the word 'myth' stems from a root which means 'utterance'. The clash between 'scientific' attitudes and the 'regressive' or 'magical' attitudes ascribed to so-called primitive cultures (with which the poetic and artistic elements of our own culture often side) is less a clash between real and illusory, efficient and inefficient, ways of dealing with the world than a clash between two different mythical systems, the first of which tries to repress any consciousness of its mythical dimension. As Elisabeth Sewell puts it:

> The only choice for the mind lies not between mythology and logic, but between an exclusive mythology which chooses to overlook the body's participation and an inclusive mythology which is prepared in varying degrees to admit the body, the notion of the organism as a whole, as a partner in that very odd operation known as thought.

Myth, in its deep structure as well as in its superficial content, is *about* this compound relation between body/mind and word/world. It is metaphoric, not in the sense that it uses what we call 'figures of speech', mere rhetorical devices, but in the root sense of the word: 'carrying across' the convenient boundaries we establish between sexes, seasons, species and stars. This metaphoric leakage is not consciously contrived, nor is it peculiar to myth; it penetrates, in the act, everything we do, all the sense we make – even in the most narrowly specialized branch of science. Our being-in-the-world is itself a continuous process of two-way criss-crossing between ourselves and the world which cannot help being metaphoric, so that, in Emerson's words, 'The whole of nature is a metaphor of the human mind.'

What is elemental is in fact extremely complex; nowhere does this appear more fully than at the very point of creation. If myth refuses to keep to the subject, to treat things purely and simply, this would account for many of the apparent inconsistencies that crop up in creation myths: for example, Sun, Moon and Stars may be described in terms of a human family and its relationships before men themselves have actually appeared on the scene. This original complexity of creation stems from an impossible unity beyond all human distinctions, a *coincidentia oppositorum*, something like the point envisaged by André Breton 'from which life and death, real and imaginary, past and future, communicable and incommunicable, height and depth, are no longer seen as contradictory'. This mutual correspondence between inside and outside, human and natural, is developed strikingly by many myths whenever an activity of fundamental import is in question. Among the Dogon, for example, weaving, planting and making love are regarded as different forms of 'speech', and all of them are implicated in the carrying-out of any single one: speech itself is a reproduction of the original 'words' of creation.

Frances Yates has observed that: 'The basic difference between the attitude of the magician to the world and the attitude of the scientist towards the world is that the former wants to draw the world into himself, whilst the scientist does just the opposite, he externalizes and impersonalizes the world by a movement of will in an entirely opposite direction.' Yet even in the realm of experimental physics Werner Heisenberg has shown that the scientist's presence is bound to be reflected in his experiment. For all its tough-minded stance, and despite the elegance of its mathematical formulations, science has not solved but only postponed the question of the origin of things. The biochemical script for the origin of terrestrial life – from the first flash of atmospheric electricity into an oceanic soup of nucleic acids, to the subsequent development, by the laws of quantum chemistry, of self-replicating molecular systems – demonstrates the logic of the elements' combination, but depends upon a purely mechanical account of their origins. The search for 'fundamental' particles produces more and more entities which lie on the edge between theory and fact. The substantiality of matter itself is in question: Heisenberg suggests that 'for modern natural science there is no longer in the beginning the material object, but form, mathematical symmetry'. And even mathematics may be not so much the *lingua franca* of the universe as an archetypal basis common to the realms of both matter and psyche, a property of what Jung called the *unus mundus*. Science is equivalent to myth, not only in function but in some of its methods of exposition. The models, the structures which scientists use are borrowed from each other's disciplines; they cross-fertilize cybernetics with biochemistry, psychology with economics: they engage in the very type of swopping that Lévi-Strauss has called 'makeshift' (*bricolage*) in myth. Ecology is the prototype of a new, holistic vision of science, which will recognize these involuntary metaphors and acknowledge, in the way myth does, the symbolic as well as the symbiotic nature of our earth-household.

Inner and outer

If it is true, as Novalis suggested, that 'The Self – considered under the categories of quantity, quality, causality and substantiality – is perhaps the object of the various sciences', then it is much more obviously one of the

The modern biochemical theory of the origin of organic cells is, on the surface, quite un-visionary: yet this photograph of the kind of electrical discharge by which nucleic acids (the building-blocks of protein) have been generated in laboratory experiments shows in its structure the same centrifugal pattern as a mandala. (Lichtenberg figure.)

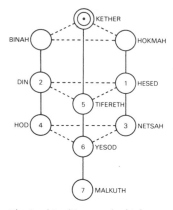

The Sephirothic tree: the highest triad (Kether, Hokmah and Binah) corresponds to the level of the transcendental 'world of emanation'; the triad beneath that, to the ideal 'world of creation'; the triad below, to the spirit 'world of formation'; and the final Sephirah, Malkuth, to the 'world of the (made) fact'. The tree can also be divided between the right-hand side – that of 'grace' or 'mercy', and the left – that of 'law' or 'rigour': the central axis is thus the 'middle pillar' which mediates between the two. The seven lowest Sephiroth are sometimes identified with the seven 'days' of creation.

Drawing by seven-year-old Kate Machin showing a cosmic dragon with the earth, sun and moon as its eggs.

objects of most creation myths. Production, division, reproduction, etc., are all processes which have an inner and an outer reference simultaneously. The Hawaiian cosmogony, for example, begins with a list of beings which are named as generalized creative processes: 'Te Ahanga: the swelling of an embryo in the body . . . Te Apongo: appetite . . . Te Kune Iti: inner conception . . . Te Kune Rahi: preparation. Te Kine Hanga: the impulse to search. Te Ranga Hautanga: ordering, as of cells in the body', and so on. There is a parallel between the creation of the cosmos and the coming-to-life of an individual. In the Indian *Shatapatha Brahmana*, for example, there is an explicit correspondence between the year which Prajapati spends within the golden cosmic egg and the length of gestation for horses, cattle and humankind. Wherever creation is thought of as a continuous process, rather than a once-and-for-all event, the correspondence between microcosm and macrocosm, visible and invisible, becomes deeper and more complex: the original pattern of creation still in-forms all creatures, especially man. In the Jewish Kabbalah the symbolic image of the Tree of Life, with its ten Sephiroth, functions as a complex and multivalent model. It serves to explain the order and interrelation of the forms of divine emanation which constitute the cosmos; it is a diagram of the principal organs and faculties of man's physical body; and it also symbolizes the various 'lights' which are within him. Furthermore, to each of the four gradations of divine emanation, the lowest of which is the 'world of fact', there corresponds a part of man: his pure and uncreated being, his spirit, his soul and his body.

Man's own creative powers can thus be seen as a version (or re-version) of the power that creates and sustains his existence. His being-in-the-world is a continuous process of re-creation, an expression of that 'primary Imagination' which Coleridge held 'to be the living power & prime Agent of all human perception & as such a repetition in the finite mind of the eternal act of creation in the infinite I AM' (a reproduction of which can be formed by the poetic exercise of the 'secondary Imagination'). Each new person's vision of the world is not a passive taking-in, but an active re-vision. Martin Buber wrote of the child's entry into life: 'He has stepped out of the glowing darkness of chaos into the cool light of creation. But he does not possess it yet; he must first draw it truly out, he must make it into a reality for himself, he must find his own world by seeing and hearing and touching and shaping it.' Potentially, everybody can re-experience himself or herself as a world-creator in this way: it is possible for the normal boundaries between one's ('subjective') self and the ('objective') world to be suspended. In certain circumstances this feeling that the universe stems from oneself can become acute: under the influence of LSD, one of Masters and Johnson's subjects reported: 'I am the nuclear image of eternity. . . . I am the original stuff.' A 'schizophrenic' patient of Roheim's stated: 'I started sunshine. At my birth I produced it, along with atoms, light and warmth. At the beginning the universe was a canoe, in which I alone had a place.' Such an explosion of the self is conventionally disapproved of, or dismissed as megalomania or paranoia; but it is a vital ingredient of poetic creation, and is grudgingly allowed under the aegis of 'artistic licence'.

Just as in certain creation accounts man is the focal point of the cosmos, in some way completing or making sense of it, so the artist can be seen as a

co-operator in the process of creation. The alchemist Michael Scotus wrote that 'whereas God is the only source of Creation Itself, a born creature may provide certain other bodies with their requisites and so guide them to their natural and most pure ends'. Like alchemy, art involves creation on two planes at once: it is a re-formation of the self at the same time as it is the formation of an object. In a sense, every artist is engaged in the elaboration of an individual mythology: certainly the images that recur in his life work tend to reflect the themes which appear in creation myths. Particularly frequent are images of a disintegration of the self: a 'chaos', that is, a breaking-down of conventional social, sexual and cultural definitions which can lead to a fresh and 'original' identification with the world, or any of its parts.

Since every person's life is, consciously or unconsciously, a creative evolution, it is not only artists who are confronted with the dynamics of creation. One aspect of the growth of personality is the process of individuation, of which the followers of Jung speak in cosmic terms: the separation of consciousness from unconsciousness, of 'ego' from 'non-ego', being a psychic reproduction of such cosmogonic scenes as the separation of light from darkness or the parting of Father Sky from Mother Earth.

This parallel between the pattern of individual life-processes and that of creation as a whole also means that the character assigned to the cosmos determines the (inner) meaning it will have for man, and consequently the part he will play in it. Sometimes, as we have seen, this role is important and co-operative: in many American Indian myths man is only one part in the

The Sky-Goddess Nut arched over her twin the Earth-God Geb. They are frequently shown held apart by the Air-God Shu. (Papyrus of Tamienu, Egypt, c. 1000 B C, British Museum, London.)

whole of creation; in our own Book of *Genesis* man is the apex, the focal point of creation (and, correspondingly, the Christian attitude towards the material world is more ambiguous). But in some cosmogonies creation almost frowns on man: for the Aztecs, the cosmos was highly vulnerable and insecure and men were bound to offer their blood, or even their lives, in order to sustain it. In other cultures the natural world is considered of little real importance: for many Hindus the whole drama of creation is indeed merely theatrical; a performance which, once its message has been understood, is no longer necessary – 'As a dancer stops dancing after displaying herself on stage, so Nature stops, after having shown herself to Mind.'

The fact that creation myths 'place' man in the universe, or act as models of processes in human, as well as cosmic, life, is reflected by the particular circumstances in which they are recounted. On the simplest level, the efficacy of a medicine may depend upon the correct recital of its (and, by implication, the world's) origin. In a more complex fashion, the creation account may function, as the Maori cosmogony does, as an analogue for all human inspiration: it is ceremonially recited to cure sterility, to cheer men's spirits and in connection with rituals of war, baptism and death, among others. As the etymology of the word 'myth' implies, the speaking/writing/acting-out of a creation 'myth' is more than a rehearsal; it is the occasion for a *re-creation*, a confirmation of the essential relations between man and the world.

Horizontal and vertical

In its telling, in the oral or written tradition by which it comes down to us, a creation myth appears first and foremost as a narrative: a sequence of events which unfolds in the space/time of a text. This 'story' is the explicit, 'horizontal' dimension of creation accounts; and it has its own pattern of jumps, loops, knots, etc. An example of a narrative loop occurs in Hesiod's *Theogony*: Father Sky (Ouranos) refuses to lift himself off Mother Earth (Gaia), allowing his children no breathing-space, until Kronos castrates him; but Kronos himself imprisons his own children, born of Rhea, by swallowing them, until Zeus in turn outwits him. Sometimes these patterns are due to attempts to edit or re-construct a myth (usually slanted in favour of one

Traditionally, each stage of the Genesis narrative is allotted an anagogical parallel. Thus, the creation of light is taken to signify the creation of the angelic hosts; and the division of light from darkness signifies the separation of good angels from bad through the fall of Lucifer. ('Bible Moralisée', France, c. 1450, Bodleian Library, Oxford.)

particular interpretation): such interference often has the effect of damping off the resonance of a myth and making it too 'transparent'. More frequently, the intricacy and peculiarity of a creation myth are the result of a collective distillation: a long and invisible succession of shapings to which our notions of personal authorship and authority cannot apply. In some cases the narrative weave of a myth has been orally transmitted for generations with an astonishing fidelity. Among the Zuñí Indians, for example, the human representative of the deputy creator god Kiaklo is the memory-bank of all 'beginning talk': in one myth Kiaklo descends to the Lake of the Dead and is instructed by the Council of the Gods: 'As a woman with children is loved for keeping unbroken the line of her kin, so you, tireless hearer, will be cherished by us and worshipped by men for keeping unbroken the stories of creation and all that we tell of past days and future.' In other cases, mistakes, corruptions and misunderstandings have almost erased the outline of the original story.

A myth is even more vulnerable to misinterpretation when it is translated from one culture to another. Most 'primitive' languages are highly sophisticated, but quite different in syntax and vocabulary from our own. Their range of association is richer and more complex by nature; in fact, it seems that the older a language is, the more deeply metaphoric its ingredients are, in that denotations which we carefully separate into abstract and concrete are simultaneously present. The hymns of the *Rig Veda*, for instance, many of which deal with cosmogonic themes, are written in an archaic Sanskrit rich in implicit meanings which often have to be read on several levels at once. Hence, what appears to be a straight-forwardly intelligible 'plot' may be rich in 'understood' meanings, and the shifts and folds of its narrative structure may be far more than devices for interest's sake. The problem of reading creation accounts is not only a technical or linguistic one; the very process of exegesis depends on the fact that the structures of language have a metaphoric relation to other life structures. Thus, in addition to their horizontal narrative dimension, the ingredients of a myth make vertical connections with other layers of meaning.

It is obvious, for example, that the seven 'days' of Creation in the first of the two accounts in *Genesis* (I:1–II:4a) are not days in the ordinary calendrical sense – the division between day and night does not appear until the fourth day – but indicate a sequence which is metaphysical or symbolic, and which can be understood only by reading *through*, or between the lines of, the literal text. In the exegetical tradition of the Kabbalah such interpretation reached extraordinary depths of complexity and subtlety, sieving through a sacred text word by word. So dense in significance, so concentrated were such texts thought to be, that they were considered, in the more daring forms of Kabbalistic speculation, as reservoirs of all possible meanings in the world, and hence as an embodiment of the original powers of creation: when copying the *Torah*, Rabbi Meir was warned: 'My son, be careful in your work, for it is the work of God; if you omit a single letter, or write a letter too many, you will destroy the whole world.'

Any major sacred text – and particularly one having to do with creation – has a multiple correspondence (which need not be consciously intentional)

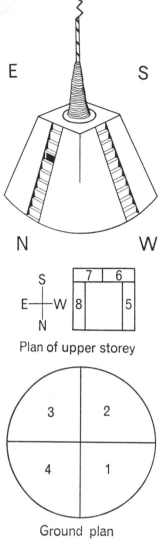

E   S

N   W

	7	6
S E─┼─W N	8	5

Plan of upper storey

3	2
4	1

Ground plan

The 'Granary of the Master of Pure Earth' is the vehicle in which the First Ancestor fell to earth. Its overlapping symbolism is immensely complicated: each side of the 'ark' corresponds to a direction, a heavenly body and a type of creature; the North, for example, is for men and fishes. The eight compartments within the granary (the 'belly of the world') correspond to the eight grains, and the eight principal body organs; and their walls represent the skeleton. (From Griaule, 'Conversations with Ogotemmeli'.)

with other, non-verbal, 'texts' of its culture such as dances, textiles or kinship patterns. The architecture of the Dogon 'Granary of the Master of Pure Earth', which descended from the sky on the fourth day of creation, and on which actual granaries are modelled, was at once a representation of the eight seeds given by God to the eight ancestors, of the eight organs of the Spirit of Water, to which human organs correspond, and of a giant female figure.

Such densely packed information – agricultural, astronomical, ethological – is not equally available to all members of the group: the Dogon elders knew of esoteric meanings underneath the more common senses of gestures, drawings and speech. Since this hidden meaning is even more inaccessible to outsiders distanced by thousands of miles or years from its original context, one can try instead to reach an understanding of it in terms which are not peculiar to any one culture.

One possibility is to work from the outside in: to match astronomical rhythms and patterns, for example, against the anatomy of a myth, much as has been done with the rings of Stonehenge. Or we can move on to middle ground: for example, the structural correspondences that Lévi-Strauss has established between the framework and career of a large number of South American myths and socio-cultural categories show an organizing process at work, a matrix of binary contrasts which he believes coincides with the neurological pattern of human intelligence. By applying these keys, myths from different groups can be decoded in order to show their fundamental solidarity. Even more than the 'reading' of the Kabbalah, the deciphering of such deep structures may involve considerable manipulation of the text and is often arbitrary or obscure.

No less so is the psychoanalytic approach, from inside out, where myths, like dreams, are seen as being determined by unconscious fields of force which are vaster than individual consciousnesses: the 'archetypes' of Jung are universal formative structures which programme the emergence of particular images into consciousness, and which also provide keys to the interpretation of myth.

I cannot pretend, within the limits of this text, to present the continuous 'reading' of a myth according to even one of these methods; this would in any case be unsatisfactory, since my aim is to suggest the diversity and complexity of meaning that such readings can yield, without considering any single method as conclusive. Myth, like poetry, pays compound interest on each re-reading. Instead, I have chosen a series of 'cross-sections'; samples of comparable moments from a coherent range of myths which demonstrate both the fundamental processes of creation and the way in which they telescope into one another.

Something from nothing

The world *is*; it is irresistibly present: how do we account for its existence? Working backwards through evolution, hauling in the chain of cause and effect, we arrive at the notion of an original 'some-thing': but what lies behind that primordial presence? A blank, an emptiness; the *absence* of 'nothing'. We can only refer to it in negative; as one Pyramid text has it,

Modern astronomers believe that stars are still being created, as dense clouds of dust (appearing as dark patches in photographs) cool and contract within a larger area of gas: the nebula (a word first coined by Kant to describe the uniform cloud of particles out of which the solar system was supposed to have condensed). (Photograph of the Great Nebula in Orion.)

'When Heaven had not been born, when Earth had not been born, when men had not been born, when the Gods had not been conceived, when Death had not been born . . .'. The more empty, the more absolute 'nothing' is, the more potent, the more radical the act of creation appears. Since 1215 the idea of such a creation *ex nihilo* has been a part of Roman Catholic dogma; but the nature of this creation has been a matter for argument. The medieval concept was of continuous creation: William of Ockham, for example, held that every moment God made each creature anew. It was probably John Buridan, in the seventeenth century, who was the first to suggest that once God had set the world in motion it would be self-sustaining. Significantly, much the same option seems to exist in modern cosmology: between the 'big bang' or evolutionary model, according to which the present universe had a definite and explosive beginning (and will have an equally definite and implosive end), and the 'steady-state' model, which accounts for the universe's expansion by a continuous creation of matter. Since a Papal Encyclical of 1951, the Catholic Church has supported the first model, on the grounds that it shows that 'creation took place in time. Therefore, there is a creator; therefore God exists'.

This uncompromising divorce between being and non-being, between something and nothing, is a typically Christian view of the cosmos: many Oriental religions see their relation as complementary instead. The Taoist philosopher Chuang-Tzu puts it this way:

> There is being. There is non-being. There is a not-yet-beginning-to-be-non-being. There is a not-yet-beginning-to-be-a-not-yet-beginning-to-be-non-being. Suddenly, there is being and non-being. But between this being and non-being, I really don't know which is being and which is non-being.

This paradox situates the origin of creation beyond the argument of being and non-being, in an inconceivable unity, the impossible point of contact between finite and infinite: chaos. In fact, the word for 'chaos' in most creation myths seldom denotes a void: in the *Ch'ien*, a commentary on the

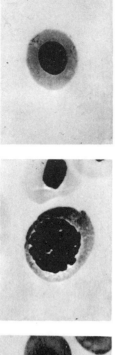

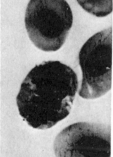

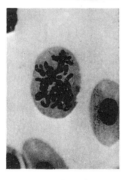

I Ching, it is written: 'When energy, form and matter are present but not yet separate, we call this chaos. . . . If one looks, there is nothing to see; if one listens, there is nothing to hear; if one follows it, one obtains nothing.' In Hesiod's *Theogony* chaos denotes a 'gap' which *comes into* being; even in our own cosmography there is dispute as to whether the 'interstellar gas' (the word is derived from 'chaos') is 'something' or 'nothing'.

Chaos, then, is the state in which everything is, but so undifferentiated that nothing can be manifest in particular: it is pure entropy, an even, indifferent distribution of energy. The world as it is, with all its distinctions, must therefore be anti-entropic, a constant assertion against chaos: Rabbi Bunam wrote that 'The universe is always in an uncompleted state, in the form of its beginning . . . it requires continuous labour and unceasing renewal by creative forces. Were there a second's pause by these forces, the world would return to primeval chaos.'

The creation of any thing entails the obliteration of this chaotic fusion. There is a story in Chuang-Tzu of how the South and North seas used to meet in the no-man's-land of Hun-Tun (whose name means literally 'mixed up'); in gratitude for his hospitality they decided to open seven orifices in him, so that he could hear, breathe, etc., like everyone else: the drilling of the last hole killed him. Another example of this obliteration of the state preceding creation crops up in our own cosmography: it has been suggested that we cannot verify the 'big bang' hypothesis because 'All traces of a previous state would have been erased by the high pressures and temperatures.' Thus, in order for creation to unfold, there must be a disintegration, a separation within the primal totality such as occurs in the division of a cell. In the Lurianic strain of Kabbalism it is held that the space within which creation took place was made by a 'contraction' of the divinity: nothingness is therefore *within* God. In Gnostic speculations the materialization of creation is thought of as the result of a breakdown of original unity (the pleroma), a fall which is occasioned by the disruptive nature of desire. According to Valentinus, Ennoia ('grace') was originally contained, along with every other thing, within Autopater (the Great Father of All); but she 'willed to break the eternal bonds and moved the Greatness to the desire to lie with her', thus initiating the materialization of the world. In any event a kind of doubling-back is involved, whereby a single totality gives rise, through an act of will which may assume its own authority, to space, time and matter: to the distinctions and qualities which are the nature of created things.

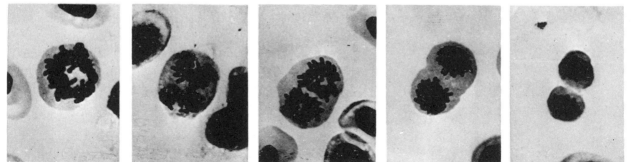

The moment of creation thus often has the ambiguous, almost tautological character of a narcissistic or incestuous act: a *Pyramid Text* tells how

> *yes I*
> *it was me*
> *grabbed my cock*
> *drained seedwater*
> *through my fist back into me*
> *I wrapped myself around cock*
> *joined in fucking my shadow*
> *fanning me under his cloud*
> *I rained seedwater*
> *spewing it like barley from the earth*
> *into my mouth my own*
>
> *I sprouted windman Shu*
> *I dropped raingirl Shefnut.*

This process of creative self-consciousness may, on the other hand, take a quite abstract or conceptual form: production by the sheer power of thought. The Zuñí creator Awonawilona 'conceived in himself the thought and the thought took shape and got out into space, and through this it stepped out into the void, into outer space and from this came nebulae of growth and mist, full of power and growth'.

On whatever scale it works (individual or universal), the creative impulse has as its mainspring energy or 'heat'. As we have seen, this impetus towards manifestation frequently has the character of desire, and hence it involves itself in a dialectic between identity and difference, which can take the form of a multiplication of 'selves' and their subsequent copulation. In the *Brihadaranyaka Upanishad*, Purusha, the Primal Man, finds no pleasure in being alone, so he divides himself into male and female and the two halves couple. 'She' thinks: 'How can he embrace me after having produced me from himself? I shall hide myself.' And so she transforms herself into various kinds of animal, through each of which the couple procreate the different species.

In some myths the 'other half' of the creator is missing, or present only in a shadowy form, without which, nonetheless, the supreme creator cannot carry out his programme: in one Eskimo myth Father Raven is the agent of creation, but he is accompanied throughout by a sparrow and at the end of the account it is said: 'Thus Father Raven created the earth, but the little sparrow was there first.' Very often, as we shall see, it is the original creator who disappears once his work has been accomplished, or who sacrifices himself in order that it should be complete.

To imagine an original whole from which such division or multiplication took place is to conceive of a time before 'time', a cosmos existing as a single, stable concentration of energy. Just as the disintegration of a 'fundamental' particle may involve the transformation of 'energy' into 'matter', so that new (and more fundamental) particles are created, so the breaking-open of the cosmic nucleus does not merely release, but effectively *creates* the opposites which constitute the dynamics of the universe. The physicist Lemaître put forward the model of such a 'primeval

The whole body of all beings-in-the-world (further images are contained in a hollow in his back) is shown here, in what is usually supposed to be a figure of Tangaroa, greatest of the gods. (Central Polynesian statue, BM, London.)

Left: *The process whereby a new cell is created (mitosis). The dark granules of chromatin collect within the cell nucleus in the form of chromosomes: each chromosome splits lengthwise into two, and the halves migrate to opposite sides of the cell, after which the nucleus divides in two. (Microphotograph of mitosis in the white blood cells of a frog, from Jirovec, Boucek and Fiale, 'Life Under the Microscope'.)*

atom' which originally existed in perfect equilibrium, but which some disturbance tipped into expanding to the size of the present universe. A parallel concept is that of the cosmic egg: an image which establishes the analogy between the production of the macrocosm and the microcosmic reproduction of humans, animals and plants from eggs, germs or seeds. In the Orphic cosmogony, for example, the silver egg of the cosmos gave rise to an ambiguous figure:

> When Time and wailing Need
> split the ancient egg
> outstepped Love the first born
> fire in his eyes
> wearing both sexes
> glorious Eros
> father of immortal Night
> whom Zeus swallowed and brought back. . . .

Out of the cracked egg come all the opposites, of light and dark, male and female, love and strife: the actions and reactions which energize the structure, in space, time and particularity, of the created world.

The conjugation of opposites

Difference is the motive force of creation: its mainspring depends upon the tension between opposites. The Sumerian word for 'universe', *an-ki*, actually means 'heaven-and-earth', and the creation or 'naming', of man cannot take place until the two have been separated. In some myths the discrimination and spacing of elements is gradual: the Japanese *Nihongi* states that 'of old, heaven and earth were not yet separated and the In and Yo [Yin and Yang] not yet divided. They formed a chaotic mass like an egg which was of obscurely defined limits and contained germs. The purer and clearer part was thinly drawn out and formed heaven, while the heavier and grosser part settled down and became earth.'

The making of such distinctions, and the consequent clearing of a middle ground between them, may require considerable force, as in the story of Kronos (see p. 10), or the Maori account in which Earth and Sky are violently separated when their children seek to 'discover the difference between light and darkness'. This divorce of the creative couple is an opening-up process which enables their offspring to see each other for the first time: 'It was the fierce thrusting of Tane which tore the heaven from the earth, so that they were rent apart and darkness was made manifest and light made manifest as well.'

In some myths the dialectic is more complex: in the *Rig Veda* Indra takes part in the conflict between Adityas ('releasers', led by Varuna) and Danavas ('restrainers'), agreeing to split the latter's leader, the great serpent Vrtra, and release the waters it has pent up. In the course of so doing, Indra swells to such a gigantic size that he forces apart his parents, Sky and Earth. (In this version, although he has insisted on being made king of the gods, Indra plays no further part in creation; the birth of the sun from the cosmic

According to the doctrine of the Orphic mysteries, the creator of the world – Phanes/Dionysus – was born from out of the silver egg of the cosmos. Here the egg is shown entwined with a spiral serpent, representing Time as the boundary of the created world. (plate from J. Bryant, 'Analysis of Ancient Mythology', 1774.)

In this diagram the occult and manifest aspects which were originally combined in God are articulated by descending into the created world. The five circles show: top, God as the combination of dark/occult and light/manifest qualities; above left, the darkness of the abyss; above right, God revealing his light out of darkness; centre, the Spirit of God floating upon the waters as the divine power creates the world from informal matter; bottom, hemispheres of Day (in which God is Apollonian, the source of beauty, harmony, etc.) and Night (in which God is Dionysian, the source of severity, punishment, etc.) (Robert Fludd, 'De Philosophia Moysaica', Frontispiece, 1638.)

waters, and man's creation therefrom, are under the supervision of Varuna.) In the Kabbalah, too, the structure of oppositions is more elaborate: each of the ten Sephiroth contains the germ of its opposite, through which it must pass before manifesting itself as the next Sephirah, to which it stands in a complementary relation. The two sides (left and right) of the Sephirothic Tree stand for 'rigour' or discrimination, and 'grace' or unification, respectively. The ground of creation is thus the middle, *between* all opposites.

In the earliest of the Chinese legends of the giant P'an Kou, he is described as a mediator between Yang (sky) and Yin (earth): 'P'an Kou, who was in the middle, transformed himself nine times each day: sometimes a god in the sky, sometimes a holy man on earth.' The distance between earth and sky widens progressively as these transformations take place; it is the mutual impact of opposites that is the motive force of creation. In the creation account of the Ngadju Dyak, the clouds, hills, sun and moon, etc., are created by the 'clashing' of two mountains. The first man and woman are made out of the debris resulting from a battle between two hornbills (another form of the same cosmic duality) in the Tree of Life, which is destroyed in the process.

No thing in creation exists in a world of its own; its very definition relates it to its negative, its opposite: disorder against order, chance against

Elohim (the word used for 'God' in the first Genesis narrative) creating Adam. In Blake's scheme of things (which was undoubtedly influenced by Gnostic thought) this imposition of a mortal coil was the work of a demiurge (Urizen) rather than of the true God. So that 'Adam is only the Natural Man & not the Soul or Imagination.' (The Creation of Adam, coloured monotype by William Blake, England, 1795, Tate Gallery, London.)

necessity, mutation against repetition, destruction against creation. As William Blake put it: 'One portion of being is the Prolific, the other the Devouring . . . the Prolific would cease to be Prolific unless the Devourer, as a sea, received the excess of his delights.' Whatever original unity may be supposed behind it, as far as the phenomenal aspect of creation is concerned duality appears to be fundamental. In one Hindu myth, Brahma makes several mistakes in the course of creation: he creates Ignorance and throws her away, but she survives; he creates Night, and she gives rise to creatures of darkness against which he is thenceforth forced to struggle. The obstruction, the resistance, of darkness and negativity are a *sine qua non* of creation from a human point of view, as Jacob Boehme saw: 'The One, as the Yes, is power and life and is the truth of God, or God himself. He would in himself be unknowable, and in him would be no joy of elevation, nor feeling, without the No.'

The true realization of creation (whether on a macro- or micro-cosmic level) is the moment when it becomes 'other', when it leaves the solipsistic orbit of its creator. In the course of manifestation this 'dark' side is expelled from the 'light' side so decisively that an absolute distance may be established between the world and its creator – or the power of the 'No' may go beyond a simple declaration of independence. The disobedience which results in Adam and Eve being expelled from Paradise, into the world as we know it, is prompted by an ambiguous serpent who was later identified with Satan. During the Middle Ages, Satan was developed into a more and more autonomous figure: he was the arch-rebel, the Prince of Darkness. But, as Jung reminds us, he may have started out as a shadow-figure belonging to 'the intimate entourage of Jahweh'.

As I shall show in the section on Descent, the distance between the creator and the created world is often felt to be a degradation or a fall from an original state of grace or innocence. In Gnostic imagery, the familiar Christian story of the Fall is given a subtle inverse twist. For the Gnostics the created world was an alienation, an embezzlement of divine properties by an insubordinate Demiurge who was not the true God (or by a series of Archons or 'governors'). Hence the serpent (Satan), far from seducing Adam and Eve, enlightens them as to their real nature, so that 'when they had eaten, they knew the power from beyond and turned away from their creators'. As a result they embark on the systematic recovery of all the fragments of divine light which had been dispersed in creation: the typical Gnostic project of 'gathering oneself from the cosmos' and thus escaping from the trap of a separate and exiled existence.

Creation can be a trap in a different sense: it may be a kind of cosmic ambush, a temporary pitch on which a struggle is to be fought to a finish between opposite principles of light and dark which have been in eternal contradiction hitherto. In the later versions of the Iranian cosmogony, Ohrmazd and Ahriman live in utterly separate realms of light and darkness respectively; but Ahriman somehow gets hold of a ray of light from Ohrmazd's world and seeks to possess it for himself. Ohrmazd is compelled to create space and time as the co-ordinates of an arena into which Ahriman will be lured, and, as a result, defeated in the end: it is in this third and middle terrain that human beings exist. The form of Gnosticism derived from this by Mani (which gave rise to the Manichean heresy) also entailed the belief that the two antagonists, Light/Good and Darkness/Evil, had existed *ab initio*, but held that the outcome of the struggle between them was uncertain.

The shadow-creator can be at once a rival and a caricature of his opposite. An Iroquois myth tells of the birth of twin creators: Maple-Sprout, born normally, and Tawiskaron, who kills his mother in the process. Maple-Sprout creates all good things, including man; Tawiskaron, in imitation of him, can produce only mosquitoes, crocodiles, etc: after being defeated by Maple-Sprout, Tawiskaron becomes Lord of the Land of the Dead. The Iroquois account, unlike the Iranian or Gnostic versions, acknowledges the essential complementarity of the twins: such recognition of the value of the negative, which is found in many creation myths (and was often labelled 'devil worship' by Christians) is a way of showing how, as Boehme put it, 'without poison and eagerness there is no Life; and from thence ariseth all contrariety and strife; and it is found that the strongest and most eager is the most useful and profitable: for it *maketh* all things, and is the *only cause* of all mobility and life.'

The contradictory aspects of creation are mythically combined in one supremely paradoxical figure: the Trickster, who is, in Paul Radin's description, 'at one and the same time creator and destroyer, giver and negator, he who dupes others and who is always duped himself'. The Trickster 'possesses no values, social or moral, . . . yet through his actions all values come into being'. Half victim, half hero, he acts unconsciously, because his intentions are local and immediate, while the process of which he is the instrument is cosmogonic. He is the essence of the appetitive thirst of existence, of the instinctual excess which keeps it moving, and therefore he is, as Kerényi says, 'a spirit of disorder, an enemy of boundaries, . . . a mighty life spirit.'

The Ladder of Being. The order of creation is not just an evolutionary sequence, from the simplest protozoa to the most complex mammals; it implies a subordination of the 'lower' forms of life to man. (Plate from Charles Bonnet, 'Oeuvres d'histoire naturelle et de philosophie', 1781.)

World-order and the order of worlds

The first order of the world is progressive, it is the sequence in which it is created: first this, and then that. But the world-order is also a ruling, a government of the cosmos; it is the law according to which it unfolds – even if only the abstract 'law of nature' playfully evoked by Gregory Corso as

> *Atoms & light Her law*
> *punishing evolution like bad boys*
> *with the slap of Her All-Void hand. . . .*

The very words for 'world' often hinge upon its structure in space and time: the Sanskrit word *maya*, which denotes the endless proliferation of manifested forms in the universe, has the connotation of 'measuring'; the Greek word *kosmos* applied at first to political, military and ceremonial Order – it was probably Pythagoras who first applied it to the universe. The sequence of creation (or of evolution, for that matter), the steps by which it emerges, imply a hierarchy: very often man is one of the last things to be created, because he is in some sense the end of creation (yet in many creation myths because man is created *before* woman, he is held to be her superior). The teleology of this climax may vary: in the Babylonian *Enuma Elish*, the earliest creation myth we know of, man is created to 'be charged with the service of the Gods that they might be at ease'; whereas in both the *Genesis* accounts it is clear that man was intended to rule over the rest of creation. This image of man as the apex of the evolutionary pyramid is quaintly reflected in the nineteenth-century philosopher Robinet's belief that mineral and vegetable formations which look like parts of the body are relics of nature's first attempts to achieve a human being. In the Middle Ages the divinely-appointed world order was seen as essentially stable and fixed in its categories; but by the mid nineteenth century a growing awareness of the mechanisms behind the variation within species led to the development of a more *evolutionary* picture, in which these definitions, while they might be retrospectively determined, were open-ended as far as their future was concerned. The change of image was from that of a definite architecture, guaranteed from outside, to that of a series of interlocking processes, in the responsibility for which man himself was actively involved; in which 'nature' and 'human nature' were confused.

The sense of a dialectical relation between structure and process is deeply engrained in Kabbalistic imagery. Writing about the 'shells' which the successive emanations of creation constitute, a recent commentator, Leo Schaya, says:

> It is only in the midst of creation that there exists effective separation and succession of possibilities, that is, a definite hierarchy in which every reality includes, in a determinate or active way, those which proceed from it, and, receptively or passively, those from which it issued.

The creative process, however it ends, begins as an *explanation* (literally: a laying-out) of fundamental principles: 'first things first'. In the Laws of Manu it is written that Brahma, after he was born from the cosmic egg, 'brought out from himself the Mind made of Being and Non-Being; and from the mind, in turn, the Ego, the self-centre of the world'. Here it is clearly the immaterial elements which have priority over the material elements: the five senses are intermediaries between the two. 'From there proceed the grosser elements and their activities; but as to the Mind, with its subtle parts, it is the creative part of all beings.'

Whenever the genesis of the world appears to be treated on a purely concrete level, it is important to remember that in this context none of the elements is simply 'material': as sources of all that is to be the world, they are profoundly metaphorical and beyond the distinction between physical and metaphysical. For the Indian Samhyka philosophers, the elements in their unfolding reveal correspondences with the senses: out of the void arose air (hearing); from air, fire (touch); from fire, water (sight); from water, earth (taste and smell). Or the elementary structure of the world may have a spatio-temporal layout: the various Navajo cosmogonies involve a complex correspondence between the four directions, times of day and properties such as purification, sustenance or fertility. If one 'element' is held to be

Sandpainting of a Navajo creation myth. In the centre is the ladder up which the Navaho climbed into this world. Surrounding it are the coloured bars of the four cardinal points. Upon each bar stands a figure (from left to right, clockwise); Dawn Man (East, white; Evening Girl (South, blue); Twilight Man (West, yellow); Darkness Girl (North, black). To the left of each is one of the four mountains which formed the corners of the earth, before it was stretched; to the right are the implements first used to trench and drain the earth; to the left of each one's head are the first men and women, and to the right are different forms of Coyote. In the corners between the figures are the plants which they found on earth and which they used for food and to smoke. (Beautyway, L. C. Wyman, 'Sandpainting of the Kaventa Navajo', Sante Fe, N. Mex., 1952.)

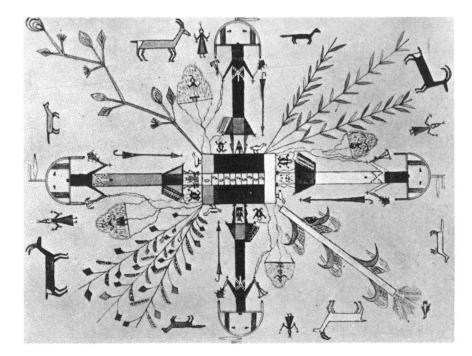

fundamental, the narrative of creation must show how the others are in effect its transmutations. In one Indian cosmogony, water is the first and only element in existence when the Highest Being sets about recreating the universe: the water stirs and a parting appears in it, making a sound which announces the presence of air/space; this wind, in its rushing, produces a friction which ignites fire; as a result of the conflagration a void is left, within which the upper sphere of heaven is established. It is only after this cosmic evolution that Brahma emerges from the centre of a glowing thousand-petalled lotus. The same process occurs in reverse when the universe is wound up again at the end of a cosmic cycle, so that water is once again the sole element.

The unfolding of a world-order may thus be cyclical in its pattern: a pattern in which decay or destruction may occupy as much space/time as creation. Sometimes the sequence is final: the whole creation may be doomed to destruction, as in the Scandinavian *Ragnarök* (where the gods themselves appear to be included in the holocaust); or else creation, having served its purpose, may be revoked, as in the Christian Last Judgment. The final moment of creation may appear as the converse, the mirror-image of its initiation; just as in physics the career or 'life' of any tightly organized concentration of energy is ultimately entropic – that is, its end state will be an absolutely average and indifferent distribution of energy: everything and nothing. On a vaster scale, however, the succession of worlds may transcend the apparent finality of disorder or destruction. In fact, Indian conceptions of numerous worlds, each with its local forms of space and time, rising and falling against a background of unimaginable cosmic 'time', have something in common with the modern 'big bang' model of the universe's origin, in which a cycle of explosion and implosion may repeat itself indefinitely. Sometimes the actual succession of worlds involves a gradual shift in the direction either of improvement or of deterioration (for, as we shall see, the world is often thought of as the reflection of an order which lies outside the known cosmos). According to the *Vishnu Purana* the first creation was of immobile things; it was dark and without intelligence; a second creation resulted in animals that were still dark and instinct-dominated: the third creation was luminous and liberated, from it resulted the Gods; but the fourth creation, which is that of men, marks a downward movement of the cycle, and is a mixture of light and dark.

In other cosmogonies the succession of worlds can be seen as a series of trials and errors culminating in the emergence of man and the world as he knows it (as in the four successive worlds of the Nahua). So that each new world shall not start entirely from scratch, a selected group may survive each destructive phase (as in the Hebrew story of Noah, or the Zuñí Emergence Myth), and carry what they have learned on into the next world. In the most recent version of the Hopi cosmogony, men live through a succession of worlds: their achievements become progressively more complex, but in each world the changes effected lead to quarrelling, greed and disorder on a new level, so that only a few still remember the creator and his plan, and, while the rest are destroyed, they are saved for the next world. The present world, Tuwaqachi, is the 'world complete'; it 'has height and depth, heat and cold, beauty and wilderness: it has everything for you to choose from'. It is such a mixture because, the easier life was made for men, the more likely they were to fall into evil ways: the Hopis therefore emphasize that 'the farther you go, the harder it gets'.

In other cases the relationship between successively created worlds may be more ambiguous: the original, primal creation may be 'digested' by a secondary creator, as Eros or Phanes and his cosmos were swallowed by Zeus (see p. 16). Many creation myths also revolve around a doubling-back in the form of a union that is at once incestuous and fertile (a notion that is, at different times and places, both sacred and forbidden): Zeus fathered Dionysus/Zagreus on Persephone, his own daughter; when Dionysus was torn apart by the Titans, Zeus burned them to ashes, and from these the human race emerged. The topology of such switches in identity or function is beautifully set out in Gary Snyder's poem 'No Matter, Never Mind':

The Father is the Void
The Wife   Waves
Their child is Matter.

Matter makes it with his mother
And their child is Life, a daughter.

The Daughter is the Great Mother
Who, with her father/brother Matter as her lover,

Gives birth to the Mind.

In such ways the original creative moment is complicated or postponed; but such processes serve also to indicate that the ultimate source of creation is of *another order*, which is difficult or impossible for us to understand, and which is quite different from the laws and orders that we have supposedly derived from it.

Descent/ascent

Many creation accounts are preoccupied with the question of what relation can exist between a changing world of finite forms and its eternal, infinite source; between the manifest and the unmanifest, or in modern terms, between matter and energy. Just as, without an effect, a cause must remain imperceptible, so according to various traditions creation is the vehicle of divine manifestation: a way of bringing God 'down to earth'. A Sufi saying runs: 'I was a hidden treasure and desired to be known: therefore I created the creation in order to be known.' In another branch of the Islamic tradition the movement of descent and its ascending reversal are dialectically linked: man has 'descended' from a paradisial state, and eventually he will not only recover but surpass it by becoming 'universal man', and thus complete the process whereby God can come to know himself.

The same image is to be found in the Kabbalah, in the *Zohar*: 'In the beginning, before shape and form had been created, He was without form and similitude. . . . But when He had created the form of supernal man it was to Him as a chariot and He descended on it, to be known.' The divine 'light' is refracted through four worlds (which exist in simultaneity), only the last of which is the 'world of the accomplished fact': the object of

Kabbalistic mysticism is to bring about the 'turning-point' which will reverse the trajectory of creation and at length restore all things to their unity in God.

This eternal, unbroken state is sometimes refered to as 'Eden'. William Blake believed that 'The artist is an inhabitant of that happy country; & if everything goes on as it has begun, the world of vegetation & generation may expect to be opened again to Heaven, through Eden, as it was in the beginning.'

In the orthodox Christian tradition, there has been a gradual shift from the early emphasis on God-the-Creator to a later concern with God-the-Redeemer; this is the reflection of a strengthening feeling that the world, though of divine origin, is fallen and corrupted in nature. The vision of creation as a loss or alienation of divine power occurs in its most pessimistic form in one Gnostic text, where it is suggested that the very shining of Divine Light into Darkness constitutes a descent, as a result of which Darkness gains temporary possession of 'sparks' from that light. The created world is the result of a fall, by which spirit is trapped or imprisoned in matter: it is the work, not of the true God, but of a Demiurge and a series of Archons 'that are lower by far than the unbegotten Father'. In a drastic inversion of the normal reading of *Genesis*, the Gnostics saw the whole sequence of creation as a struggle between a messenger from the world of Light and the forces of Darkness which seek to deceive the First Man and keep him from knowing his true nature (e.g. by confining him in Paradise). In Buddhism, too, life on earth is seen as being both tempting and degrading: when a new, sweet-smelling earth appears after the destruction of the old, radiant beings descend from Heaven; but after eating the earth they lose their luminosity, and as they decline further and further, so more and more distinctions appear: first the framework of time and the seasons, then discrimination between beautiful and ugly, and so forth. Similarly, in the Iranian cosmogony, Ohrmazd has to descend from infinite time into 'Time of the Long Dominion' in order to overcome Ahriman. (See p. 19.)

In a less fatal way the coming-to-life of any creation involves the transition from a potential and universal state to one which is actual and particular: there is a Jewish saying that 'In the mother's body man knows the universe, in birth he forgets it.' Many speculations about the origin of creation suggest that the world of created things is only a reflection – and sometimes an inept or illusory one – of an invisible, higher world. According to Plato's *Timaeus*, 'the world has been framed in the likeness of that which is apprehended by reason and mind and is unchangeable, and must therefore of necessity, if this is admitted, be a copy of something'. The Iroquois believed that every thing on earth had an 'elder brother' in the sky-realm. One of these 'Ongwe' became pregnant by The-Old-One-In-The-Sky; she was lured to a hole in the sky-realm and pushed through, thus initiating a chain of events which resulted in the formation of the world. Through such images descent is seen to be more than mere genetic succession: it involves a radical difference between what is above and what is below. In many African myths the first men are lowered to Earth from the sky; or else God withdraws from living among men on earth.

The discrepancy between the individual forms of creation and the 'reservoir' of potential life can be expressed in the form of a delegation (as

Creation is often seen as a coming 'down to earth' from some transcendent realm; a materialization which entails some form of descent. Here the fiery sphere of divine soul-stuff descends from the four-square Wisdom of God to the infant's body (to whose form it will gradually adapt) while it is still in the womb. The figures surrounding the mother carry different cheeses representing the varying quality of human seed (a demon can be seen contaminating some at top left). (Descent of the Soul, miniature from Scivias of Hildegard of Bingen, Germany, c. 1150, Biblioteca Statale, Lucca.)

When the first human beings ascend into the newly-created world, they are as children; sometimes they are actually born from out of the ground. In this Mixtec version the first man and woman climb out of a womb-tree which is opened-up for them by two divine beings, who may be playing a Trickster role, as their costumes seem to be the wrong way round. (Codex vindobonensis mexicanus 1, Mexico, Österreichische Nationalbibliothek, Vienna.)

opposed to a usurpation) of the business of creation: the Pueblo corn-mother Iyatiku creates the prototypes of all creatures in the Underworld, but her twin daughters carry out the actual planting of trees, releasing of animals from their baskets, etc.; they also appear as the mothers of human beings. The chain of command may stretch even further: in the previously quoted version of Hopi cosmogony Taiowa, the Creator, delegates the execution of his plan to Sotuknang, who creates earth, water and sky; he in turn makes Spider-Woman responsible for the creation of life, and she creates, among other things in the world, twins who are responsible for 'keeping the world in order'.

As we have seen in the previous section, the succession of worlds may take an upward instead of a downward direction: one version of the Zuñi creation account tells of four cave-wombs through which mankind is led by magical twins (emissaries of Father Sky and Mother Earth); in each of the wombs the properties and qualities of the world become more complex, until at last the present 'world of disseminated light and knowledge' is reached. In the *Popul Vuh*, when the Gods find that they cannot get animals to speak the names of their makers, successive versions of man are created out of mud, wood and rushes; finally they succeed with a mixture of corn-meal dough. In the Navajo emergence myth the stages of ascent are full of intricate cross-references: in one version, man does not appear until the Fifth World, when the Gods combine in order to create him; he is named 'Created-from-Everything' because 'They made his feet, his toe-nails and ankles of the soil of the earth, his legs of lightning. . . . They made him of all kinds of water . . . and they made his arms of the rainbow. His hair was made of darkness, his skull of the sun. . . .'

Earth-body and sacrifice

In the correspondence created between parts of his body and parts of the world, man is a microcosm, a miniature of the universe. The relation is metaphoric both ways: the world is in him and for him. He is the focus of its orbit; and at the same time he is in the world, a member of a gigantic organism whose directions incorporate his. The ecological vision of the Whole Earth is only the most recent image of a long tradition which reaches back through the Hermetic teachings to the idea of a world-soul, an *anima mundi*. Plato's *Timaeus* showed that the entire cosmos must, by virtue of its order and harmony, possess intelligence and be 'in very truth a living creature with soul and reason'. The cosmos of the *Timaeus* is framed by a creator: but in many myths the creator dissolves into his creation, in nearly all cases through death or self-sacrifice. After the Norse giant Ymir was slain by the three first gods,

> From the flesh of Ymir the world was formed,
> From his blood the billows of the sea,
> The hills from his bones, the trees from his hair,
> The sphere of Heaven from his skull.

In Hindu cosmology Purusha, the Primal Man, is dismembered and the universe is formed of all his parts. (Hence, to recognize the essential unity of macrocosm and microcosm was to lose one's particular identity in that of Purusha.) In some cases, such as the Egyptian Memphite creation account, the creator god is identified with the first appearance of earth: one of Ptah's names is 'The Uprising Earth'.

The earth is both the elementary index of creation, the first and original basis for life, and the continuous source for whatever subsequently comes into being: hence the earth is identified as the mother of all living things. In a myth of the Thompson Indians of the North-West coast of America, Earth lived up in the sky at first, but because she complained of the Sun's ardour, the Old One put her below and told her:

> Henceforth you will be the earth and people will live on you and trample on your belly. You will be as their mother, for from you bodies will spring, and to you they will return. People will live as in your bosom and sleep in your lap. They will derive nourishment from you, for you are fat; and they will utilize every part of your body.

The Hopi Indians believe that the Earth reveals herself most specially in the form of the Corn-Mother, for corn is 'a living entity with a body similar to man's in many respects, and the people build its flesh into their own'. This cycle of transmutation not only runs across living genera, it is sometimes involved in the process of creation itself: by his self-sacrifice the creator is dispersed or diffused throughout creation; but he may be continuously resurrected, for example in plant form. By eating these plants men play their part in the circulation of the creator throughout his world. The paradox that the creator is present *because* of his self-sacrifice is parallel to the idea that human death (which often appears at the same moment in the myth) is part

Even when a creation is fated to come to finish, its creatures must offer life to the source of life. Tonatiuh, the sun (left), carries under him the date of his inevitable end; standing under the moon, upon the jaws of earth, a demonic version of Venus (Tlauixcalpantecuhtli) offers him a sacrifice of quail's blood. (Codex Borgia, Mexico, 15th c., Biblioteca Apostolica Vaticana, Rome.)

of a larger-than-lifetime cycle. Amongst the Ceram of New Guinea the primordial beings were called Dema; one of these, Hainuwele, who had been born from a plant, was ritually murdered by the first men. Her dismembered and buried body gave rise to various plants, many of which were valuable as food. But another Dema made the first men go through a ritual dance, in which they passed through a door made of Hainuwele's arms; as a result some became mortal and sexed human beings, others turned into animals.

In some accounts the sacrifice upon which creation depends meets with more resistance: in the *Enuma Elish* it is not until Marduk has defeated Tiamat that her body can be split into earth and sky; and the idea of wresting benefit from the earth by force is perhaps reflected in the fact that the same word, *ku-bu*, which applied to Tiamat's dismembered parts also referred both to the foetus and to metallic ore. In the Aztec cosmology the function of sacrifice is effectively reversed: Quetzalcóatl and Tezcatlipoca forced the Earth Monster Tlalteutli to come down from the sky; but she proved so ferocious in her appetite that they had to tear her apart. Everything – earth, sky, gods and living forms – was made from her, but she remained insatiable: 'She is the Goddess who sometimes weeps at night, longing to eat human hearts, and she refuses to remain silent so long as she is not fed, and she will not bear fruit unless she is watered with human blood.'

Death, time and the elements

The condition of life, the return for its changing nature, is death: whatever is created and grows by transmutation must follow the descending arc of the cycle through decay and death (though who knows whether death itself might be not just an occasion but a process as extensive as life?) Death is the obverse of the self-preserving, appetitive drive or 'desire' of all living organisms: it can therefore be seen as the hidden mainspring of the created world. In the *Brihandaranyaka Upanishad* it is written that 'In the beginning there was nothing. Everything was enveloped by Mrtyn [Death], by appetite, for appetite is death. Then he [Mrtyn] thought: "If only I could have a self." And reciting praises, he began to move. And while he was reciting praises the waters came into being.'

Similarly, the descent into a world locked in time and space, which we have seen in many accounts of creation, is sometimes depicted as a fatal attraction. In the Gnostic *Poimandres of Hermes Trismegistos*, Primal Man is drawn into the power of the sevenfold planetary Harmony through his infatuation with Nature: to disentangle himself, he 'shall recognize that he is immortal and that the cause of death is love'. The Gnostic idea that man must, as it were, decant himself from the created world reappears in Jung's claim that 'we die in such measure as we do not distinguish'. In other words, death, as the ultimate dissolution of identity, is the dialectical contrary of the process of individuation which is characteristic of human life.

In many myths, as we have seen, Death is presented as a figure opposite, but *complementary* to, the Creator as source of life. Sometimes the darker, misguided twin of the creative pair turns, after his defeat, into the Lord of the Land of the Dead, as was the case with Tawiskaron; or the impetus for creation may come from the Underworld, from which all living things emerge and to which they must return, as was the case with Iyatiku: death is the invisible obverse, the missing link in the cycles of created life. The myth of Hainuwele shows that without death and distintegration the cycle on which fertility depends cannot proceed; and the association of edible plants with sexuality shows that the same rhythm governs human life as well as vegetable life. The time without death is thus a time before sexual distinction; just as the primordial man is often a-sexual or bi-sexual. Birth and death are the beginning and end, less of matter or energy themselves than of the individual, personal forms taken by them. In the well-known *Genesis* story, the discovery of sexuality is coincident with that of death, and both are a reflection of the partial and particular situation of man-in-the-world.

The Land of Youth, which appears frequently in folk tales, is a land free from death, disease and want, in which there are no signs of change, neither of decay or growth – hence the impatience with it of those few mortals ever admitted there – but, above all, it is a land of life suspended out of time. Time is another of the conditions which bracket the created world. Some myths attempt to distinguish between a local or mundane time and a universal, cosmic time: it is in terms of such a time that the length and succession of Kalpas (world-eras) is reckoned in Hindu cosmology. The idea that Time is in some way the ultimate arbiter between the opposing principles which motivate the cosmos was expressed by the Greek philosopher Anaximander:

> The original of all that exists is the infinite, and whence is the coming into being for all that exists, thereunto also their destruction takes place as is fitting. For to each other they pay fine and compensation for their deviations, according to the ordinance of time.

In most creation accounts, however, the provisional nature of time is underlined. In Iranian cosmology Ohrmazd was forced to create a world in time, thus 'contaminating' his integrity: 'And that he might reduce the aggressor to a state of powerlessness, having no alternative he fashioned forth Time. And the reason was this, that the Destructive Spirit could not be made powerless unless he were brought to battle.' In the *Enuma Elish*, once Marduk has overcome Tiamat, he proceeds to establish the zodiac and the seasons as the framework of time, within which his creation is contained. And in *Genesis* the pattern of time on earth is created on the third 'day' through heavenly bodies which act as signs, not only for hours and seasons, but for the existence of a law and order behind appearances: in the tradition of the Apocalypse, the revocation of creation, and the consequent end of time, will be signalled by extraordinary motions of these bodies.

The end of the world is a return to the elements, not only in that it will be reduced to its fundamental constituents, but also because the order of things is reversed, and the element which accomplishes the destruction of the created world is often the one which originally gave rise to it. Water is probably the element most often chosen as the 'ground' of creation; and correspondingly, there are more than five hundred recorded myths which tell of the destruction of the world by some kind of flood (even if there may be a chosen minimum of survivors to carry life over into a new or renewed world). In Egypt, it was Nun, the watery chaos, that Atum stirred into life: Apsu and Tiamat, the primordial couple of the *Enuma Elish*, are identified with fresh and salt water respectively. For the Greeks of Homer's time, Okeanos was the watery 'origin of all things' that encircled the world and formed the boundary between known and unknown: the eight Nummo spirits of Dogon cosmology are also called 'water'.

We have already seen how earth was often considered as the primary element: similar claims have been advanced for fire and air. These 'elements' are by no means elementary: it is not their chemical properties which matter, but their metaphoric complexity. Gaston Bachelard has evoked the multiple significance of fire:

> Of all phenomena, it is really the only one to which can be applied so neatly the two contrary values: good and evil. In paradise it blazes; in hell it burns. It is kind and tormenting: it is cookery and apocalypse. . . . It is a protective and terrible deity, good and bad. It can contradict itself: it is therefore one of the principles for universal explanation.

The multivalent aspects of the elements lead them into a transmutative cycle, in which they change into each other in the course of creation. The simplest example is the relation between the elements of a duality such as the Chinese Yin-Yang: Chou Tun-I wrote that 'the Great Ultimate through movement generates Yang. When its activity reaches its limit it becomes tranquil. Through tranquillity the Great Ultimate generates Yin. When tranquillity reaches its limit, activity begins again.' This circulation of elements is the most fundamental version of the dialectic between life and death, between the free and bound states of energy. The same forces which inform a thing during its life continue beyond its death with their own recurrent rhythm: according to Heraclitus, 'Fire lives the death of air, and air lives the death of fire; water lives the death of earth, earth that of water.'

In the making

In most creation accounts that are specifically concerned with them, the elements simply appear; they materialize of their own accord. But myths which recount the beginning of the world in such impersonal terms are a minority: most accounts focus, if not on the agent, then on the *action* of creation. When Goethe's Faust was trying to translate the opening of St John's gospel he finally hit upon the formula: 'In the beginning was the deed.' Yet a magician like Faust must have known that of all the actions by which creation is accomplished – moulding, planting, weaving or carving, for example – one is pre-eminent: speech.

Language stands on the threshold between doing and a 'thought' we cannot speak of. Language is a ragged cloak for the world, and yet over and over again men have seen their speech as a reflection, or even a reproduction, of another more fundamental articulation: the world as the script of a divine utterance.

אב אג אד אה או אז אח אט אי אכ אל אמ אנ אס אע אפ אצ אק אר אש את
בג בד בה בו בז בח בט בי בכ בל במ בנ בס בע בפ בצ בק בר בש בת
גד גה גו גז גח גט גי גכ גל גמ גנ גס גע גפ גצ גק גר גש גת
דה דו דז דח דט די דכ דל דמ דנ דס דע דפ דצ דק דר דש דת
הו הז הח הט הי הכ הל המ הנ הס הע הפ הצ הק הר הש הת
וז וח וט וי וכ ול ומ ונ וס וע ופ וצ וק ור וש ות
זח זט זי זכ זל זמ זנ זס זע זפ זצ זק זר זש זת
חט חי חכ חל חמ חנ חס חע חפ חצ חק חר חש חת
טי טכ טל טמ טנ טס טע טפ טצ טק טר טש טת
יכ יל ימ ינ יס יע יפ יצ יק יר יש ית
כל כמ כנ כס כע כפ כצ כק כר כש כת
למ לנ לס לע לפ לצ לק לר לש לת
מנ מס מע מפ מצ מק מר מש מת
נס נע נפ נצ נק נר נש נת
סע ספ סצ סק סר סש סת
עפ עצ עק ער עש עת
פצ פק פר פש פת
צק צר צש צת
קר קש קת
רש רת
שת

In the Sepher Yetsirah God's thinking and making are absolutely identified in the process of writing: the various combinations of the alphabet have a creative, not a merely representational, power. 'But how was it done? He combined, weighed and changed: the Aleph with all the other letters in succession, and all the others again with the Aleph . . . and so the whole series of letters. Hence it follows that there are two hundred and thirty-one formations, and that every creature and every word emanated from one name.' This diagram shows the combinations of the twenty-two letters without permutation.

Because of its unique correspondence to the structure of the world – because in effect, by articulating it, it *creates* that structure – language has a power that is more than notative or descriptive. In Hebrew the same root DVR can mean both 'word' and 'thing': it is not surprising, then, that some Kabbalists held that the Hebrew alphabet was the one used by God as a medium for the creation of the world. It is written in the *Sepher Yetsirah*: 'Twenty-two letter-elements: He outlined them, hewed them out, weighed them, combined them and exchanged them, and through them created the soul of all creation and everything else that was ever to be created.' The *Torah* (or law) was considered to be a degraded or garbled version of the original, primordial *Torah* out of which God had summoned the world: Gershom Scholem tells us that it was even suggested that 'the sections of the *Torah* are not given in the right order. If they were, everyone who reads in it might create a world, raise the dead and perform miracles'.

A comparable attitude towards the sacred power of writing can be found in Islam: a commentator on the *Koran* refers to a gigantic tablet upon which Allah has written all that will happen until Doomsday: 'God looks at this tablet three hundred and sixty times a day. Each time He looks at it, He gives out life and death, He exalts and abases, He honours and humiliates, He creates what He wants and decides what seems good to Him.'

In other accounts it is the living utterance of the word that unlocks the power of creation. When Prajapati hatched out of the cosmic egg, the first words he spoke were 'Bhuh, Bhuvah, Svar', which brought into being the earth, the aether and the sky. (The repetition of these words is still part of the ritual of an orthodox Brahmin.) In the *Popul Vuh* the first real men are given life by the sole power of the word: 'It is said that they only were made and not formed, they had no father, they had no mother. . . . They were not born of woman, nor were they begotten by the Creator, nor by the Maker, nor by the Forefathers. Only by a miracle, by means of incantation were they created and made by the Creator.'

The first *Genesis* narrative, too, describes the stages of creation as a series of divine *fiats* in which thought and power, idea and realization, are identical and simultaneous. The primal identity of word and deed is shown by the fact that each of the womb-chambers of the Navajo emergence myth is called a 'speech/action'. In other myths (and in the rituals connected with them) the chanting or singing of sacred formulae is necessary in order to bring things to life: in the most recent of the Hopi cosmogonic myths, after Spider-Woman has created the First Twins, she creates all the forms of life on earth, including men, and animates them by covering them and singing the Creation Song over them. The sacred songs of men on earth are seen as a reflection of this original (just as the Polynesian cosmogony was believed to have a revivifying effect); when they can no longer be heard, then it is time for the earth to be destroyed again.

Singing, planting, weaving, moulding, carving, etc., are all actions that bring something into being, or lay the ground for that process: it is inevitable that men should believe that the first moment of creation was the original of such actions, a magnified, superhuman version of the knowledge they imply. Many African myths refer to God as the moulder or constructor of the universe, and the second *Genesis* narrative tells how Jahweh-Elohim created Adam (whose name means 'red dirt') 'out of the dust of the ground'.

There is at least a phenomenological truth in this, in that the nature of the world as we know it is marked, not only by man's material techniques, but by his use of language. The very word 'poetry' comes from a root which means 'to make'. The structure and dynamics of language do not simply reflect the activities and patterns of man's life; they percolate right through them. The profound metaphoric correspondence which links all of them together is developed with a marvellous complexity in the Dogon cosmology. The work of creation is accomplished by a series of 'words'. The first word constituted a process, that of weaving a covering for the Earth's womb; the second was associated with the coiling fertility within that womb; and the third was built into the structure of different types of drum. For the Dogon, therefore, weaving, agriculture, dancing and sexual intercourse (for example) are all forms of 'speech' which reproduce the original words of creation. The first men, like new-born children, could not speak: the gift of words was the gift of articulation, not just because of the expressive capacity of language, but because the first 'words' brought with them the eight grains and all the conditions required for their cultivation.

This idea of 'speech', in all its richness, conveys a sense of the world as an immense texture of different articulations which interlock with each other by analogical or metaphoric correspondence: the created world speaks to man because he is bound to look behind the evidence of all its various parts for a significance which is specifically addressed to him. The words which he hears vary from one culture to another, but the closest to us come from our own tradition in the writing of Hildegarde of Bingen:

I am that supreme and fiery force that sends forth all the sparks of life. Death hath no part in me, yet do I allot it, wherefore I am girt about with wisdom as with wings. I am that living and fiery essence of the divine substance that flows in the beauty of the fields. I shine in the water, I burn in the sun and the moon and the stars. Mine is that mysterious force of the invisible wind. I sustain the breath of all living. I breathe in the verdure and in the flowers, and when the waters flow like living things, it is I. I found those columns which support the whole earth. . . . I am the force which lies hid in the winds, from me they take their source, and as a man may move because he breathes, so does a fire burn but by my blast. All these live because I am in them and am of their life. I am wisdom. Mine is the blast of the thundered word by which all things were made. I permeate all things that they may not die. I am life.

RIG VEDA X. 129

Was neither Being nor Non-Being then,
Neither Air nor Space beyond.
What was it, forcefully stirring? Where? In whose keeping?
Was it water, deep beyond sound?

Was neither Dying nor Undying then:
No sign to mark day from night.
Breathless, breathed ONE, by his own motion:
Other then That, was nothing.

First: Darkness covered by Darkness.
The Universe an invisible wave.
Then, by Heat's power came ONE,
Empty, from out of the void.

Desire, to start, was its growing;
Desire, the first germ of Mind.
Poets, seeking by reflection in their selves
Made out, within Non-Being, Being's thread.

Acrossways stretched their line.
Below, what? What above?
Sowers and powers there were,
Self-stirring below: Self-Sacrifice above.

Who knows for sure, who here could tell
Whence born, this realization, whence issued?
Gods came later, results of this production . . .
Where That itself comes from, who knows?

This creation, where it came from,
Whether a foundation or not,
He who surveys from highest heaven,
Alone knows – unless He knows nothing about it?

The relation between infinite and finite, between the world as we know it and whatever may lie, invisible to us, beyond it, is one of the central problems that any account of creation has to deal with. The motifs of the central field of this Ushak rug are cut off by the border in an asymmetrical and apparently arbitrary way, giving the impression that the pattern of the field extends beyond and under the border. This is almost certainly a deliberate device intended to symbolize the contrast between the Boundlessness of Allah and the limits (or 'frame') of human perception. (Ushak wool star carpet, Western Turkey, 18th c.)

In the Christian tradition the usual image is of a world created *ex nihilo*: brought into being through the absolute power of God's word. The spirit of God, symbolized by a dove, and released by the creative *fiat*, circumscribes an area of Being from out of the darkness of Non-Being (right). By the same power that created the world God can also destroy it: the waters from which the earth emerged on the third day of *Genesis* can also submerge it, when God repents himself of his creation. In Bosch's image (above) the creator is outside the terrestrial sphere, with

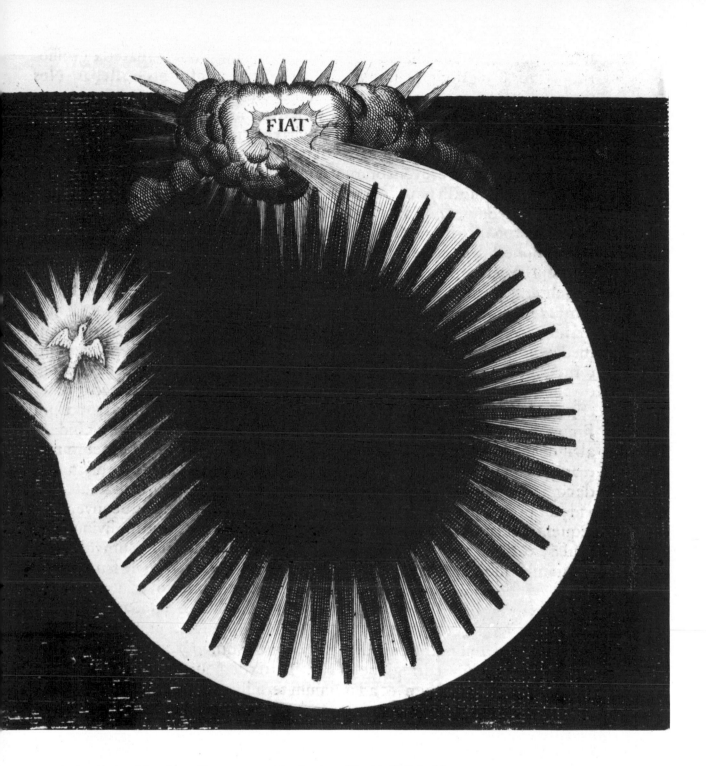

the inscription 'He said and it was done; he commanded and they were created', and in a deliberate ambiguity the world is portrayed *both* as it was originally and as it was restored after the Flood (the two events being typologically connected). (Outer wings of the triptych 'The Garden of Earthly Delights', by Hieronymus Bosch, Netherlands, 15th c.; plate from Robert Fludd, *Utriusque cosmi . . . historia*, Oppenheim, 1617-18.)

Quod homo secreta dī ñ debet
plus scrutari. quā ipse uult manife
    Quod filī dī nat° in   ſſtare.
mundo morte ſua diabolū ſupauit
ᴉ electoſ ſuos ad hereditatē ſuā re⸗
    Verba oſee de eade re. ſſduxit
    Qd corp° filū dī in ſepulchro
p̄ triluu iacens reſurrexit. ᴉ homi

iń uia ueritatis de morte ad uitā
oſtenſa ē.   ſſdū eoſ apparuit·
    Qd̄ filī dī a morte reſurgenſ. di
cipulis ſuiſ frequentᷓ ad corroboran⸗
    Qd̄ filio dī aſcendente ad pa⸗
tᷓ. ſponſa eī diuerſiſ ornamtiſ ſun⸗
                  ſſdataē:

To Christians this world is not only a creation brought down to earth: it is, as a result of the first disobedience, a *fallen* creation, and it entails an eschatology in which all will finally be redeemed. In the centre of this early medieval miniature the six days of creation (running from left to right, in pairs) are shown, penetrated by a silver 'finger' stemming from the golden disc which encloses the blue circle of the Holy Spirit. To the right of this, Adam is shown refusing to smell the white flower of obedience and falling into darkness as a result. At the bottom the dawning light of the Blessed Virgin Mary appears, with Christ rising out of it and darting flames against the satanic darkness, in order to rescue the Old Adam. (The six days of creation, page from ms. of *Scivias* by Hildegarde of Bingen, Germany, c. 1150.)

In order to obtain his supernatural powers, the shaman must return to the source of creation. Here it is symbolized by the divine rock-crystal, reached via a spiral path which has on it the mountains of the four quarters (to the right at the bottom of the path) and the curtain of sun-rays (wavy lines above these) through which he must pass. Like the project of the alchemist, the shamanistic ascent (or descent) is a *real imaginary* journey beyond any distinction between inner and outer. (The shaman's quest, wool-yarn and beeswax painting by the Huichol shaman Ramón Medina, Mexico, 20th c.)

'In the beginning Elohim created the heavens and the earth.' In the mystical tradition of Christianity, the first of the two *Genesis* accounts has been interpreted as a manifestation of the ' "noumenal" or spiritual universe of Real Being in terms of its eternal, archetypal Ideas': it is only in the second ('Garden of Eden') version that this primary manifestation is in turn translated, in terms of movement and form, into the universe as perceived by the senses.

For the poet Blake, on the other hand, the world as conceived by Reason is unnecessarily limited by comparison with the world of imaginative perception, and is therefore the work of 'Urizen' (from a Greek word meaning 'to bind'). His image of the Creator, though strikingly similar to the early medieval one, is opposite in meaning: Urizen is a caricature of God, an almost Gnostic demiurge. Hence, 'Error, or Creation will be Burned up, & then, & not till Then, Truth or Eternity will appear.' (God as architect of the universe, miniature from ms. of *Bible moralisée*, France, 13th c.; Ancient of Days, watercolour by William Blake, England, 1794.)

The initial gesture of creation can be conceived of as a mark or 'trace' which sets up a primal division, thus establishing a 'figure' from out of the ground of chaos. A number of paintings by the American artist Barnett Newman refer explicitly, by their titles, to this first moment of genesis. Their archetypal format evokes a correspondence between the creation of man and man's own creative process: the rich colour of this example can, incidentally, be connected with the fact that the Hebrew word *adamah* means 'red dirt' – the earth out of which the first man was made. (Adam, painting by Barnett Newman, USA, 1951–52.)

The earth is the body of creation: the word 'matter' comes originally from the same root as 'mother' (the Aryan *ma*: to measure, build or construct). The Earth Mother produces an endless variety of forms of being through her fertility, and takes back their used bodies: 'energy' is continually circulating through 'matter' and migrating from one form or state to another. Dubuffet's painting shows the earth as a coagulation of shapes; half embryonic, half fossilized – a kind of biological compost. (Natura Genetrix, painting by Jean Dubuffet, France, 1952.)

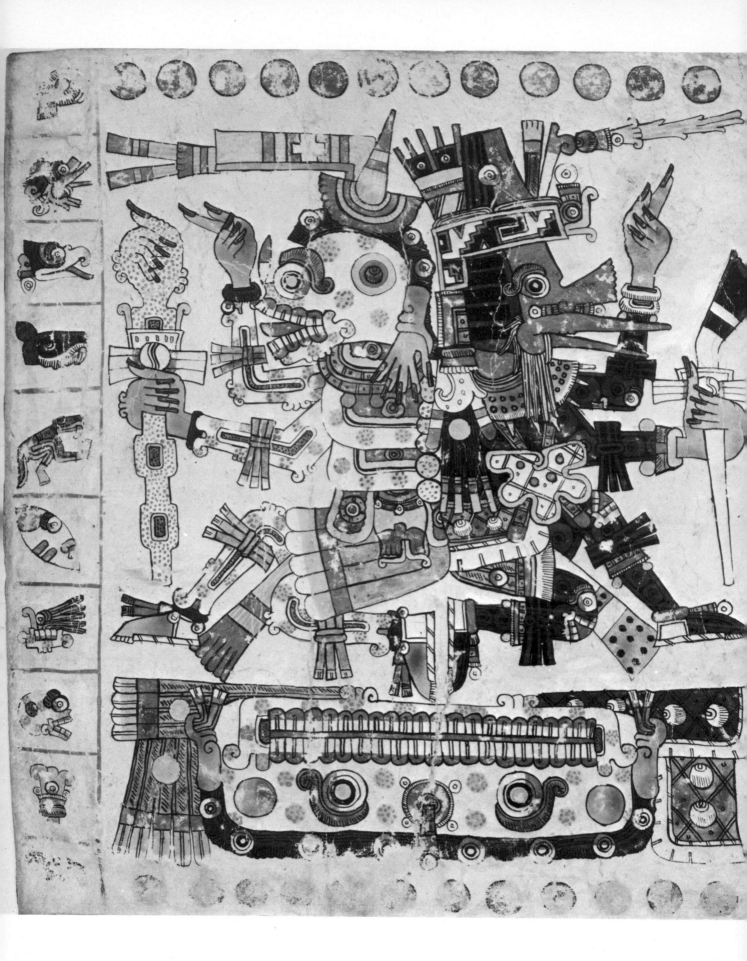

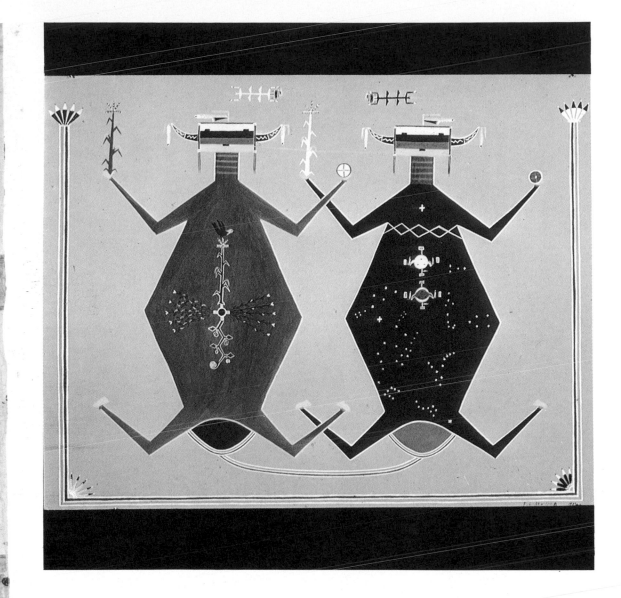

Creation is a setting-into-motion, a circulation of energies: its additional surplus actually depends upon a corresponding subtraction. Life and Death (like Blake's 'Prolific' and 'Devouring', see p. 18) are not so much separate forces as different facets of the same process. Quetzalcóatl (here in his aspect of wind god and animator) and Mictlantecuhtli (the skeletal god of the dead) are the conjoint lords of the time-span of human life (represented by the twenty day-signs on either side of them). (Page from ms. *Codex Borgia*, Mexico, c. 15th c.)

To the intercourse of sexual opposites – father and mother – upon which the creation of human life depends, corresponds the conjugation of opposites on a cosmic scale – sky and earth, for example. In this Navajo sandpainting, Father Sky carries signs for the Sun, Moon and Milky Way; Mother Earth carries signs for the four sacred plants, growing from a central lake of pure water (which also signifies the place of emergence): both wear red bars marking the life-principle on their necks. (Sandpainting from the Navajo Hail Chant, USA, 20th c.)

St Hildegarde of Bingen's vision of the cosmos is, as it were, a Christian mandala (only in reverse order; see illustration on right). In the inner circle of the terrestrial globe are the four elements (blue/water; gold/fire; green/air; black/earth); surrounding it are the celestial waters containing the west wind; surrounding this is the aether and its stars, ruled over by the Moon (with Mercury and Venus above), with the east wind at the bottom; surrounding this is a fiery darkness with hail and lightning, at the left of which is the north wind; this in turn is surrounded by a region of clear fire which contains the Sun (with Mars, Jupiter and Saturn above), and the south wind at the right. (The universe, miniature from ms. of *Scivias* by Hildegarde of Bingen, Germany, c. 1150.)

The mandala is a sacred diagram which displays the structure of the universe. The Sanskrit word means 'circle/centre': each time the mandala is meditated upon, the pattern is reconstituted whereby an original, central deity (in this case Vairocana, 'The Illuminator') gives rise, by successive emanations, to the full complexity of a world-order. (Mandala of Kunrig, Buddhist *tanka* on cloth, Tibet, c. 15th c.)

The world-order is often a hierarchy of levels of being, or 'worlds', extending from creation (or sometimes from a point below it: 'Hell') up as close as possible to the source of creation: the vanishing-point (or *nirvana*) where there is no distinction between what is manifest and its origin. The central circle here consists of twenty 'worlds' (indicated by rectangular captions), within a sacred lotus which is marked with the four directions and floats upon an ocean. Stemming from the lotus is a scale of twenty further 'worlds', the uppermost being that of blessedness and clarity. (A chart of the Majestic Worlds of the Flowery Storehouse, rubbing from a Buddhist stele, China.)

The world-order of creation and the particular processes of human ordering (binding, marking, building, weaving, etc.) run parallel: the abstract is not derived from the concrete nor the physical from the metaphysical. Yet their relation is bound to be metaphoric, since all – even the cosmology which seeks to contain them – are incorporated in the larger multiverse of human being-in-the-world, all the parts of which correspond in continuous cross-reference. Traces and boundaries (temporal, territorial, social . . .) are often so interwoven that it is misleading to render their interconnection in terms of 'symbolism'. This Japanese platform on a pillar is constructed (using no other joint than binding) for the Small New Year festival; it is eventually destroyed in a fire-battle between two generations of males, the older on the platform, the younger on the ground. (*Do-so-jin*, photo by Günter Nitschke, Nozawa Onsen, Japan, 1975; see pp. 70–71.)

In Hindu cosmogony the Supreme
Being is both the source of all possible creations, and the link between
the succession of worlds within any
particular creation: 'from every hair
of his body a world is suspended,
and each world undergoes a certain

number of dissolutions and renovations'.

Within this cosmic concatenation each world has its own order. This world (top layer) is supported by eight elephants and eight snakes; but, 'the elephants being unable to bear the weight, the world is placed upon the head of a thousand-headed snake which is supported by Vishnu himself'. In the centre of the world Drughaswamy sits on the tail of an alligator and is in charge of the sun and moon: Brahma (Vishnu's deputy) sits at the left and 'gives directions about the creation of men, animals and vegetables'. (Pages 1 and 6 from an English transcription, c. 1800, with commentary, of murals on the walls of the Shastrum of Pier-Maal's pagoda at Madura, India.)

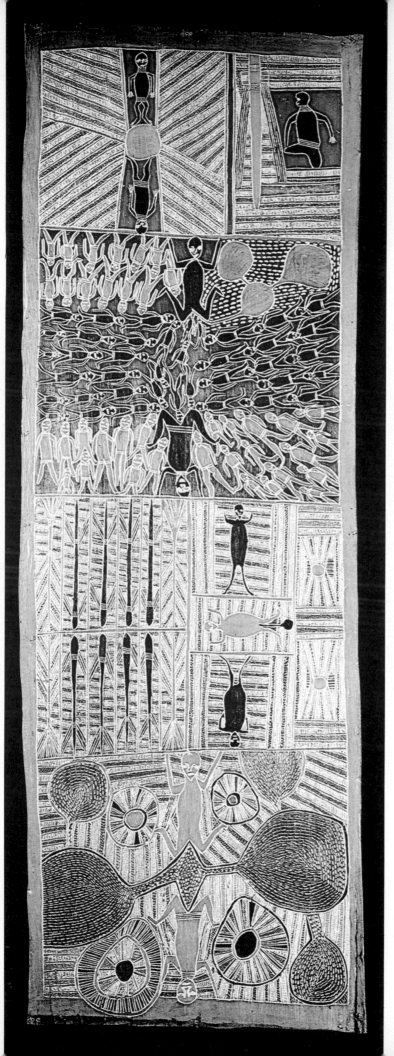

The sequence of creation constitutes a sacred order, a *hierarchy*: in many cultures (including that of the Australian Aborigines) its recital is, by the power of analogy, a rehearsal which is more than symbolic. Here (left) the artist, Mawallan, has drawn himself in the top right-hand corner reciting songs from the cosmogonic Djanggawul cycle; below him the Djanggawul sisters give birth to the first Aborigines (the same scene is repeated, more abstractly, at the bottom). Below them are the special *rangga*, the 'sacred poles' used to make the first trees; and to the right of them are the full Djanggawul – two sisters and a brother – followed by symbols for the rising and setting sun, with which they are sometimes identified.

In the Christian account the 'days' of *Genesis* are also symbolic of a divinely instituted order. In this tapestry (right) God is in the centre pronouncing the creative *Fiat lux*, 'Let there be light'; in the hemisphere above him are figures representing, from the left: the earth; the darkness on the face of the abyss; the spirit of God floating on the waters; the creation of light; and the separation of the waters above the firmament (containing the sun, moon and stars) from those below. In the hemisphere below are the creatures of air, land and water, flanked by two representations of Adam: on the right naming the animals, on the left with Eve issuing from his side. In the four corners of the enclosing rectangle are the cardinal winds; and surrounding the whole is the (incomplete) framework of the months and seasons of the year. (Gerona Tapestry, Spain, 12th c.)

The seven 'days' of Genesis can also be seen as a progressive descent from the potential or ideal world 'down to earth'. In these rare illustrations to a Jewish *Haggadah* (symbolic commentary on the Scriptures), the narrative runs from right to left. The divine emanation is re-presented by a descending fan of rays, except on the Fourth Day, when it is reversed.

Right-hand page: Above, right: the un-formed world, with the Spirit of God hovering over the waters of the abyss. Above, left: the first day; the separation of light from dark-

ness. Below, right: the second day;
the firmament dividing the waters
above from the waters below.
Below, left: the third day; the
creation of vegetation.

Left-hand page: Above, right: the
fourth day; the creation of lights in
the firmament. Above, left: the fifth

day; the creation of sea and air
creatures. Below, right: the sixth
day; the creation of animals and
man. Below, left: a personification of
the Sabbath, sitting in con-
templation. (First two pages of the
Sarajevo Haggadah, probably Nor-
thern Spain, 12th c.)

In some cosmologies creation is so closely identified with its divine source that the world is pictured as the body of God. When, in the *Bhagavad Gita*, Arjuna begs Krishna to show himself in his cosmic form, the vision is an awesome one; yet the use of this image of the all-embracing God as a Tantric icon shows that devotees must, in a converse project, have attempted to envision the universe as being within their own selves. (Vishnu-Krishna manifesting his cosmic form, painting, Jaipur, India, c. 1810.)

In this exceptional medieval drawing, the largest figure represents the Church as the mystical body of Christ in a complex iconography (in which, for example, the four Evangelists are correlated with the four directions). The body of Christ also contains, as in many medieval maps, a mundane geography (with Asia in the east at the top). (Drawing by Opinicus de Canistris, c. 1340.)

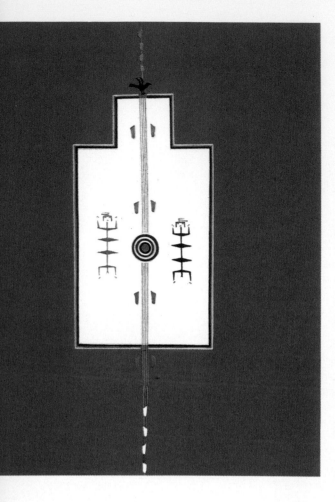

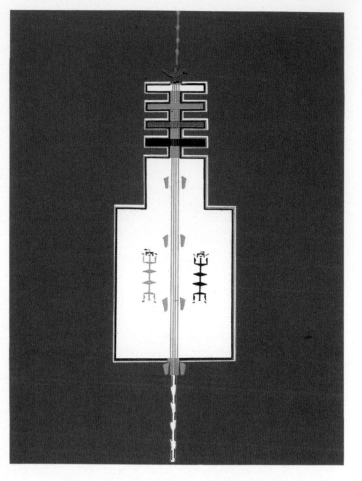

In some creation myths man's being-in-the-world, far from being a descent, is seen as the final stage of a gradually ascending series: for the Navajo this world is the fourth (and, in this case, white) world. These four sequential sandpaintings are ritually 'drawn' as an accompaniment to the chanting of sections from the Emergence Myth. They are not so much an illustration as a *re-enactment* of the stages of creation, as is shown in the very process of their construction: the ingredients of their making (cornmeal, pollen and powdered plants or flowers) are some of the sacred substances of the myth itself. And the piling of four layers of colour (black, blue, yellow and white) in the centre of the first painting is a rehearsal of the ascent through four worlds.

In the first sandpainting, the oblong shape is edged with these colours of the successive worlds: the circular shape in the centre is the place of Emergence. On either side of it are the Messenger Flies, and above it, the Blue Bird of happiness. The rainbow-path with footprints which approaches the painting from the East becomes a sacred yellow pollen-path as it approaches the centre.

In the second sandpainting the Blue Bird perches on four bars which stand for the four worlds.

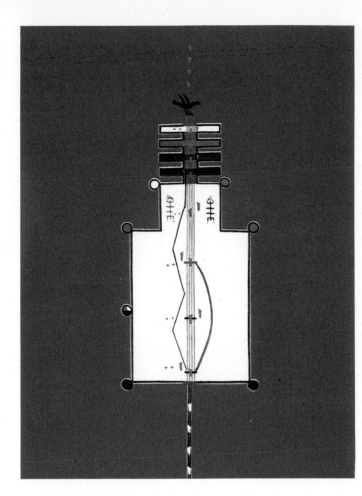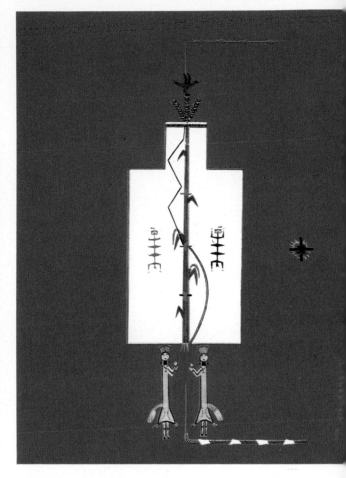

In the third sandpainting, a masculine zig-zag of lightning and a feminine rainbow-path run in parallel up the central axis. The seven circles around the edge of the oblong are the holy mountains which peg the earth down.

In the fourth and final sandpainting, the central axis has turned into a sacred corn plant, up which the male and female paths run in complement to each other. The footsteps lead into the oblong between twin figures of Fthkaynah-ashi (through whom the creator breathes his substance into the world), pass up the Tree of Life, and then turn back towards the North. (Navajo sandpaintings, USA, early 20th c.)

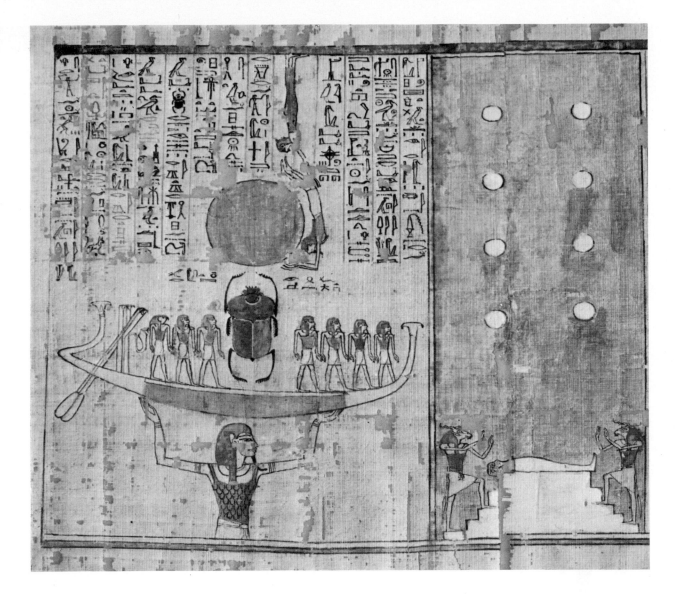

Sometimes the passage of energy into matter, and of life back into 'nothingness', is seen as a condition of suffering, a continuous sacrifice, both in birth and in death. Writing of his 'Theatre of Cruelty', the poet Antonin Artaud explained: 'I use the word cruelty in the sense of appetite for life, of cosmic inflexibility and implacable necessity, in the Gnostic sense of the tornado of life which eats shadows up, in the sense of that suffering without the unavoidable necessity of which life

could not articulate itself. . . . The hidden god, when he creates, obeys the cruel necessity of creation which is imposed on his very own self . . .' (letter, 1932). In the ceremonial sacrifices of the Aztecs, the god concerned was believed to enter into the body of the victim and thus be offered to himself. (Tonatiuh offering blood to aspects of Quetzalcóatl, page from *Codex Borgia*, Mexico, c. 15th c.)

Rising up and going down are thus

both equally essential to the movement of creation. For the ancient Egyptians the raising-up of the sun (on which the world depended) from out of the darkness of the primordial waters not only took place each sunrise, but was re-enacted in the journey of the soul through the Underworld after death. The Solar Barge, with its seven gods, is lifted up by Nun (watery chaos); Khepri the scarab in turn supports the disc which stands for the (Under)world. (*Papyrus of Anhai*, Egypt, 12th c. BC.)

For creation to be accomplished fully, it is sometimes necessary for a creator figure to descend to the Land of the Dead; to sacrifice himself, and (perhaps) be reborn. These two pages from the Mexican *Codex* *Borgia* seem to deal with the descent, sacrifice and resurrection of Quetzalcóatl in the various forms of his Venus aspect: Evening Star, Venus vanished, and Morning Star.

Top page (left-hand page of this book): From the belly of the Earth-Mother, Tezcatlipoca, flanked by two forms of Tlazoltéotl, descends to a circular 'sun-field' towards which two processions of gods are moving along blue paths. Within,

Quetzalcóatl in his black form offers blood from his pénis, and is sacrificed (the vanishing of Venus).

Bottom page: Xólotl (Venus as Evening Star) is flayed, and his heart sacrificed: Tezcatlipoca receives the blood. The body is thrown into the realm of darkness and destruction (left) and becomes a plaything in the starry ball-court (right). Xólotl boils in a sacrificial pot (bottom left); his heart gives birth to the Xólotls of the four directions (centre); and he is reborn from a shell in a twisted form (right). (Two adjacent pages from ms. Codex Borgia, Mexico, c. 15th c.)

For the individual, if not for the universe as a whole, time is finite: it has a beginning and an end, in death. The relationship between the two is shown in this unique page from a Mixtec magic book. Sixteen of the twenty day-signs are arranged about a skull set in a pool of blood, and associated in groups of four with dead gods, at least three of which can be identified as those concerned with hunting, fertility and dancing. The other four day-signs are in the corners of the square, each surmounted by the figure of a warrior-victim (possibly a captive). (Page from ms. *Codex Borgia,* Mexico, c. 15th c.)

Since the elements are the material basis for creation, they are sometimes seen as a kind of straitjacket by which spirit is confined in this world. In William Blake's visionary cosmology the conditions or 'laws' of creation are imposed by the will of Urizen, and the manifestation of the elements therefore occurs under duress:

. . . First Thiriel appear'd
Astonish'd at his own existence,
Like a man from a cloud born; & Utha,
From the waters emerging, laments;
Grodna rent the deep earth, howling
Amaz'd; his heavens immense cracks
Like the ground parch'd with heat then
*   Fuzon*
Fla'm'd out, first begotten, last born.
*   (The Book of Urizen.)*

(The Four Elements, illustration by William Blake, England, 1794.)